Japanese CANDLESTICKS ANALYSIS

"Enlightenment Through Realised Knowledge"

By: Digital Marketer

Contents

INTRODUCTION
- Historical footprints...3
- Why use Japanese Candlesticks?...4
- Intrinsic price movement and psychology...................................5
- Candlestick construction..6

CANDLESTICK PATTERNS

Single Line
- Doji...8
- Hammer...9
- Shooting star..10
- Hanging Man..11
- High Price Gapping Play/Low Price Gapping Play......................12
- Belt Hold Line...13

Two Line
- Engulfing..14
- Harami...15
- Piercing Line..16
- Dark Cloud Cover..17
- Tweezer Top/Tweezer Bottom...18

Three Line
- Morning Star..19
- Evening Star..20
- Upside-Gap Two Crows...21
- Three White Soldiers...22

- Three Black Crows..23
- Tasuki Gap..24
- Gapping Side-by-Side White Lines.......................................25
- Advance Block...26
- Abandoned Baby..27
- Rising Three Method/Falling Three Method............................28

SUMMARY
- Candlestick Pattern "Cheat Sheet"..29
- Frequently Asked Questions 30

Historical Footprints…

"Let history navigate the future"

Japanese Candlestick charting and techniques is one of the most effective ways to read price movements in the financial market. The methodology, so called because of its similarity to a candle, has been developed over the centuries in Eastern Asia.

It was originally used in Japan, during the Edo-period (1603-1868), to monitor and forecast price movements of the country"s most prized commodity, rice; which was mostly traded at the Dojima Rice Exchange near the historical commercial capital, Osaka.

Widely based on military tactics of the time, Japanese Candlestick techniques have provided traders with an edge, long before bar and point and figure charts, while evolving into a compelling strategy for today"s fast and volatile markets.

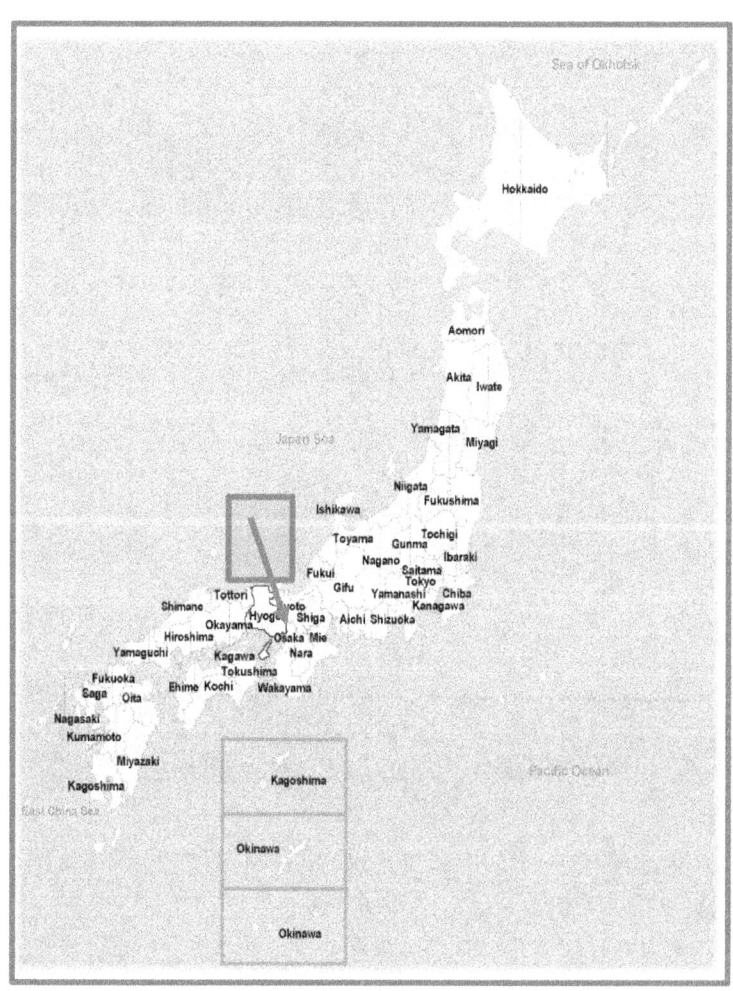

Why use Japanese Candlesticks?

"He who is well prepared has won half the battle"

Three key reasons to use Japanese Candlesticks:

- **Visual dynamics.** Japanese Candlesticks are more clear, visual and pleasing to the eye, than other charting tools, offering anyone from the first time user to a seasoned professional, an x-ray perspective of price movements and emotional health of their chosen market. This can be used to evaluate the market's perception of underline fundamental events.

- **Precision timing.** Japanese Candlesticks act as a unique leading indicator, producing superior timing for entry and exit of trades. Reversal signals can be given in ONLY a few sessions, offering a critical edge over other techniques which often require several weeks. This is what makes Japanese Candlestick techniques a more compelling strategy for today"s fast and volatile markets.

- **Enhances Technical Analysis techniques.** Japanese Candlesticks complements most other Technical Analysis techniques that you may already be using, from traditional trend, pattern and momentum analysis, to the more sophisticated Ichimoku Kinko Hyo or Demark Indicators. This is simply because Candlestick charts use the same four trading cycle data points as bar charts – open, high, low, close.

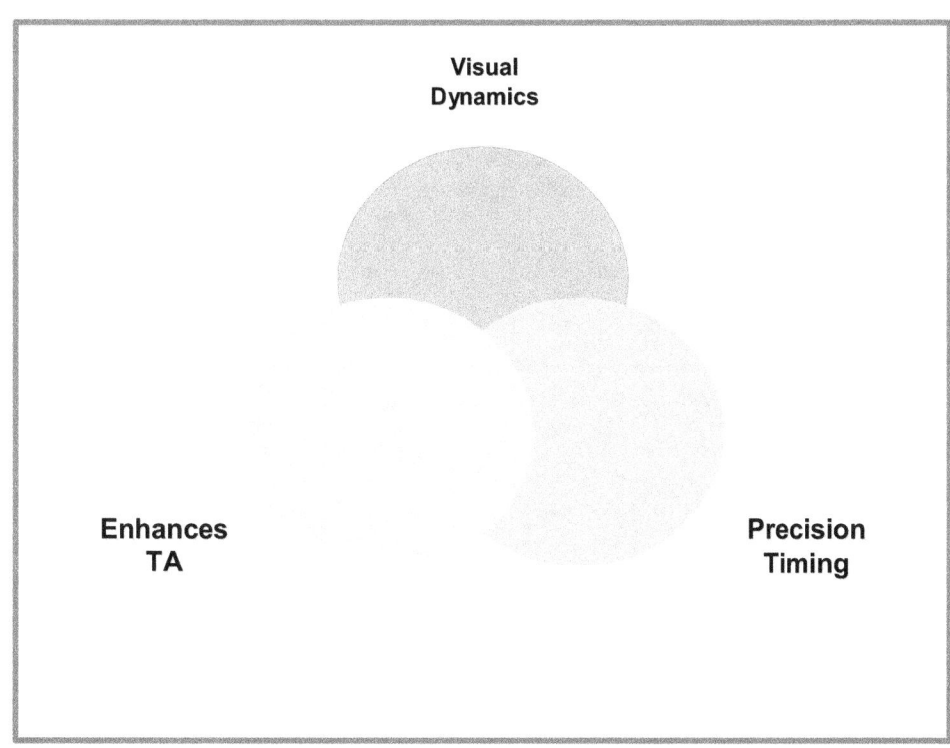

Intrinsic price movement and psychology

"A thousand mile journey begins with the first step"

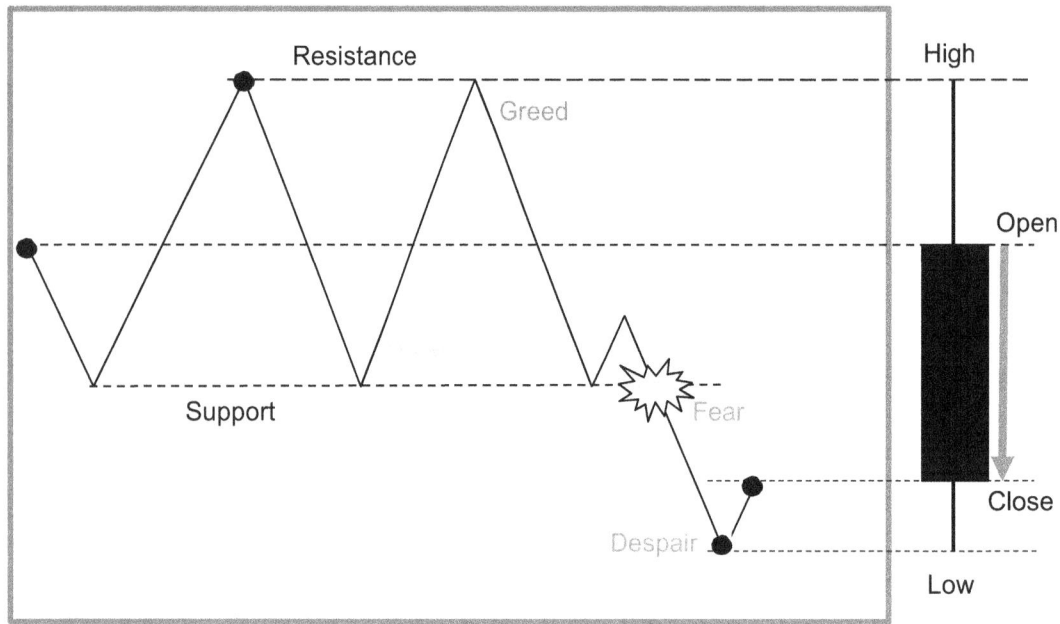

The line chart above is an example of intrinsic price movements and psychology which is crystallized in a Bearish or Black Candlestick.

- Price falls during the opening session, makes a low, then eventually pushes higher and doubles in value. At this extreme high point the number of buyers in the market diminishes, thereby creating a vacuum for prices to fall again and retrace to the previous low which had been anchored psychologically into our mind.

- Market participants, governed by their profit and loss performance, are subject to a cycle of human emotions, (hope, greed and fear).

- Assuming that we are buyers, "hope" for a reassertion higher from support, **"greed"** on the second profitable run, with instinctive expectations of a new high and last but not least, **"fear"** of potentially „getting it wrong" as price fails at resistance and **"despair"** of the unknown as price accelerates downward through support, thereafter capitulating onto un-chartered territory.

Candlestick Construction

"Simple in design, powerful in application"

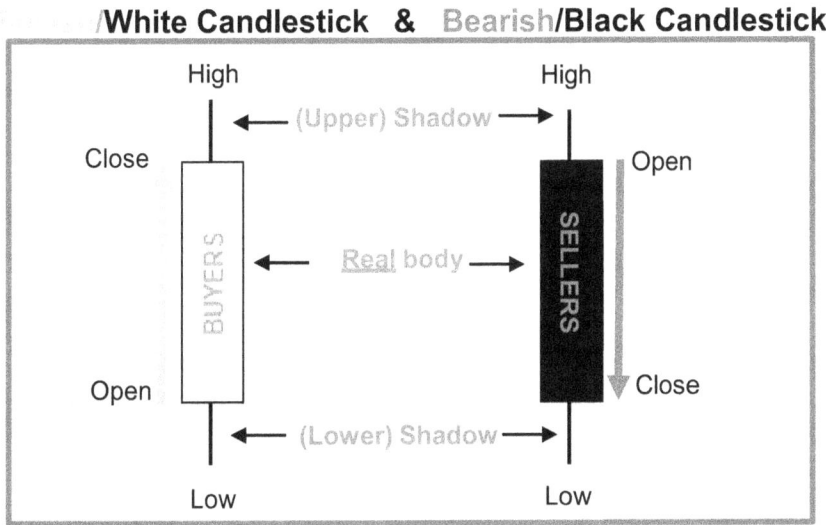

Bullish/White Candlestick & Bearish/Black Candlestick

Type {CNDL<go>} to review Japanese Candlestick signals

- A **Bullish or White Candlestick** implies that the closing price of the session was higher than the opening price. This means that buyers maintained control and prices spent more time pushing higher.

- A **Bearish or Black Candlestick** implies that the opening price of the session was higher than the closing price. This means that sellers maintained control and prices spent more time pushing lower.

- **Real Body:** The rectangle section of the Candlestick, called the „real body", is the range between the session"s open and close. The „real body" represents overall commitment in the market and what Japanese chartists describe as „the essence of market psychology".

- **Shadows:** The thin lines extending out from Bullish/White or Bearish/Black Candlestick „real bodies", are called „shadows" (upper/lower) and highlight the price extremes for the session. The „shadows" also tell us where momentum was offset.

CANDLESTICK PATTERNS: Single Session

The Doji (Doji Bike)

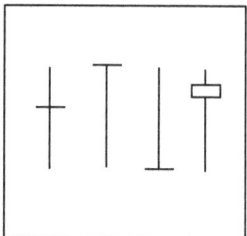

Signal
- Indecision, vulnerability, uncertainty, all of which can be considered neutral or lead to a reversal.

Criteria
- The open and close are at the same level or near.

Implication
- Paramount in identifying market tops as it is a sign of an ambivalent market, where buyers and sellers are in balance. Less implication when located in oscillating markets where it is simply confirming a trendless environment.

Fig 1. Doji marking the top of Crude oil"s impressive rise; with both 20 and 200 day moving averages exhibiting widening divergence.

CANDLESTICK PATTERNS: Single Session

Hammer (Takuri)

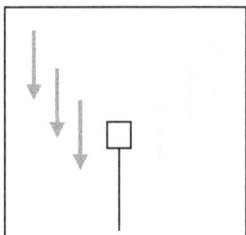

Signal
- Bullish reversal when found in a downtrend.

Criteria
- Must be located in a downtrend.
- Lower shadow tends to be at least twice the length of the real body which should be at the top of candle.

Implication
- Market is "hammering out" a bottom. The lower shadow indicates downside rejection of a price level.

Fig 2. Hammer generates a key low, following an extended decline on the Dollar trade-weighted index. Thereafter, a bottoming pattern induces signs of recovery.

CANDLESTICK PATTERNS: Single Session

Shooting Star (Nagare Boshi)

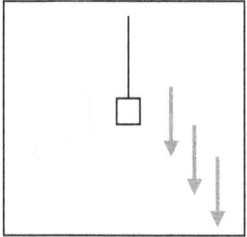

Signal
- Bearish reversal.

Criteria
- Must be located within an uptrend.
- Upper shadow tends to be at least twice the length of the real body which should be at the bottom of candle.

Implication
- Symbolizes "trouble overhead". The upper shadow indicates upside rejection of a price level. Ideally gaps away from prior real body but this is not necessary.

Fig 3. Shooting star signal highlights price exhaustion on Gold, following a powerful bull-run. The peak also marks an important final stage in Elliott Wave analysis, using Tom DeMark's TD D-Wave.

CANDLESTICK PATTERNS: Single Session

Hanging Man (Karakasa)

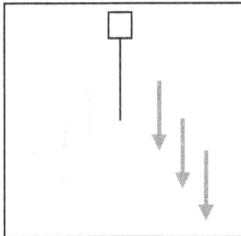

Signal
- Bearish reversal.

Criteria
- Must be located in an uptrend.
- Lower shadow tends to be at least twice the length of the real body which should be at the top of candle.
- Following session needs to confirm with a bearish candle falling within 50% of initial uptrend session.

Implication
- Uptrend was dominant force, enticing a gap higher. But sellers take control and post an intraday low. This is then reversed higher by buyers before the end of trading. A bearish candle on the following session confirms reversal.

Fig 4. Hanging man marks an important peak in US Long-term Government Yields following a breakout from a rising multi-month trend-channel.

CANDLESTICK PATTERNS: Single Session

High Price Gapping Play/Low Price Gapping Play

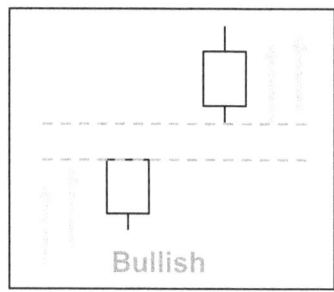

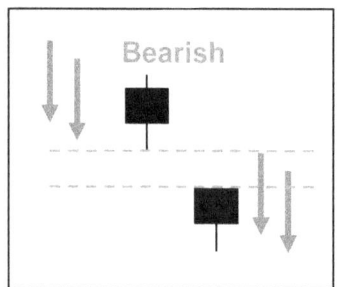

Signal
- Bullish continuation when gaps up.
- Bearish continuation when gaps down.

Criteria
- Price action is in a period of congestion near its highs (high price gapping) or lows (low price gapping), stabilizing the prevailing trend, then gaps further in the direction of the prevailing trend.

Implication
- The gap is defined as the move out either up or down, continuing the direction of the trend. It is the strength necessary to break beyond the established period of restraint.

Fig 5. The chart displays Russian Ruble in a strong downward trend. Here, price paused momentarily to collect momentum. Upon breaking through the support line which forms the bottom of the consolidation period, price gaps down, resuming the prevailing bearish move with renewed strength.

CANDLESTICK PATTERNS: Single Session

Belt Hold Line (Yorikiri)

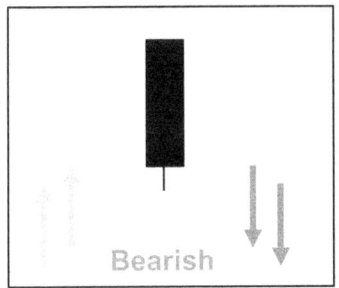
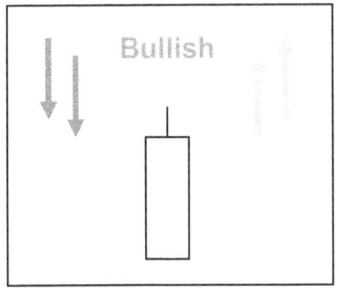

Signal
- Bullish belt hold opens on low and closes at or near high of candle after a preceding downtrend.
- Bearish belt hold opens on high and closes at or near low of candle after a preceding uptrend.

Criteria
- The body must be the opposite color of the prevailing trend.
- There must be a significant gap, no shadow at open and a markedly long body.

Implication
- Yorikiri is a Japanese sumo wrestling term meaning "push your opponent out of the ring while holding on to his belt." Most important if they are preceded by a prevailing trend and confirm resistance on the next day"s close.

Fig 6. The euro opened significantly jumped higher than the previous day"s close, then backed down for the rest of the day, closing on a long bearish candle.

CANDLESTICK PATTERNS: Two Session

Engulfing (Tsutsumi)

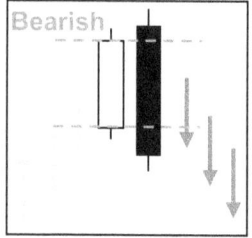

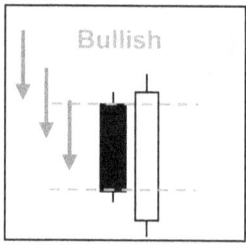

Signal
- Bearish reversal when found in an uptrend.
- Bullish reversal when found in a downtrend.

Criteria
- Must be located within respective trend (see above).
- Second real body (open & close) engulfs prior session"s real body, not necessarily the shadow.
- Second candle must be white for bullish engulfing and black for bearish engulfing.

Implication
- The engulfing indicates a transition of power between buyers and sellers, with the winner overwhelms the previous trend.

Fig 7. A series of (Bearish/Bullish) Engulfing signals at various swing points on the UK"s FTSE Stock Market.

CANDLESTICK PATTERNS: Two Session

Harami (Harami)

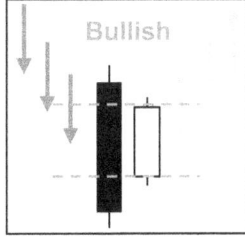

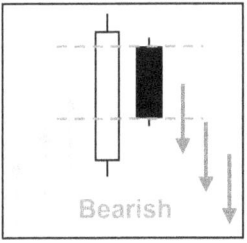

Signal
- Bullish reversal when found in a downtrend.
- Bearish reversal when found in an uptrend.

Criteria
- Must be located within their respective trends.
- Second real body is relatively small and contained within the prior session"s real body.

Signal
- The dominant force is losing power and potentially changing to the opposite direction. Pregnant or mother candle gives birth to a small candle, reversing the trend.

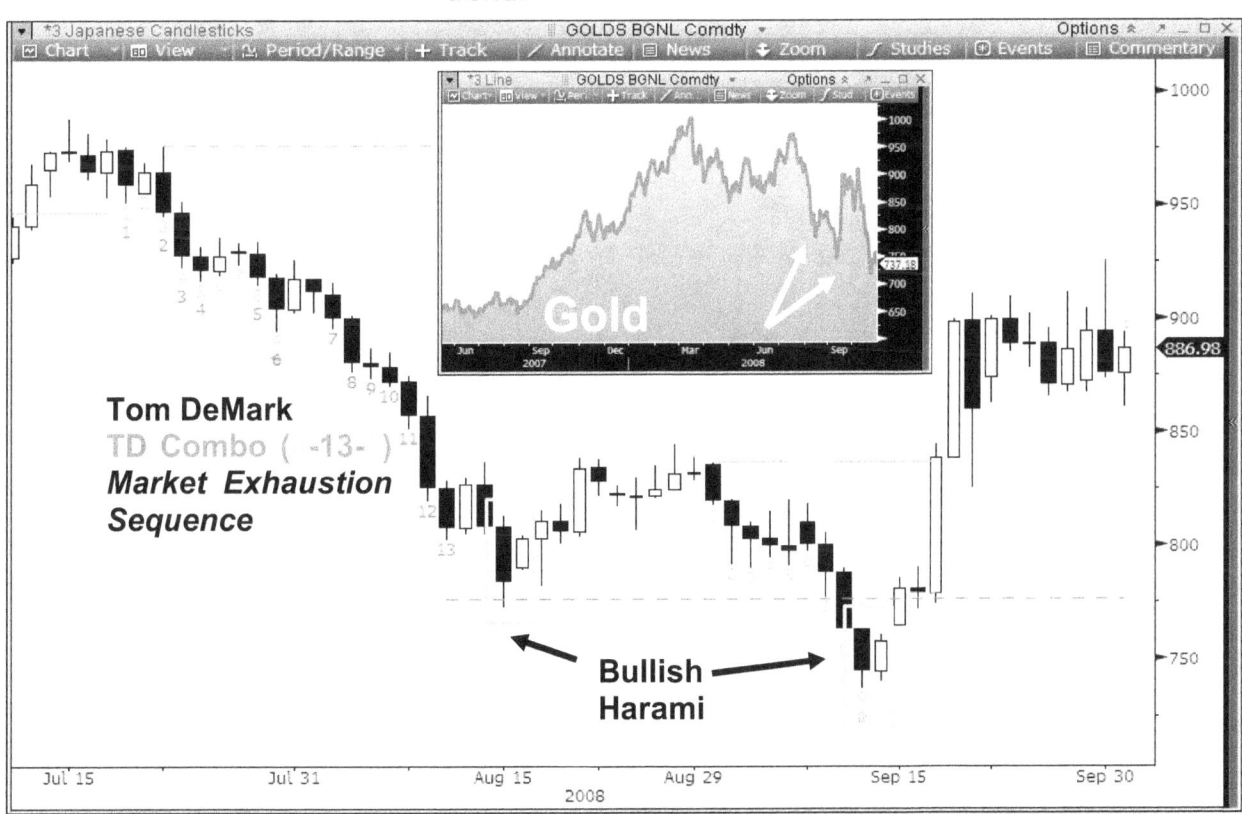

Fig 8. Harami carves out key lows, within an extreme market exhaustion sequence (9-13-9), using Tom DeMark"s TD-Combo indicator.

CANDLESTICK PATTERNS: Two Session
Piercing Line (Kirikomi)

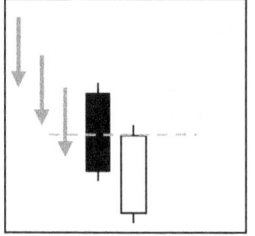

Signal
- Bullish reversal.

Criteria
- Must be located within a downtrend.
- Long bearish candle at the end of a downtrend. The following session opens lower and then reverses higher, within 50% of the prior session"s real body.

Implication
- Downtrend was dominant force, enticing prices to gap lower. However, before the end of trading there is a positive reversal, which offsets recent fall. Sellers are left questioning their position.

Fig 9. Bullish Piercing line candle pattern regaining control after a sharp decline that temporarily punctures the lower Bollinger Band.

CANDLESTICK PATTERNS: Two Session

Dark Cloud Cover (Kabuse)

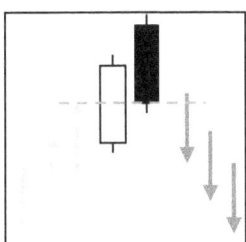

Signal
- Bearish reversal.

Criteria
- Must be located in an uptrend.
- Long bullish candle evident at the end of uptrend. The following session opens higher and then reverses lower, within 50% of the prior session's real body.

Implication
- Uptrend was dominant force, enticing prices to gap higher. However, before the end of trading there is a negative reversal, which offsets recent rise. Those who were waiting for a short opportunity can now participate.

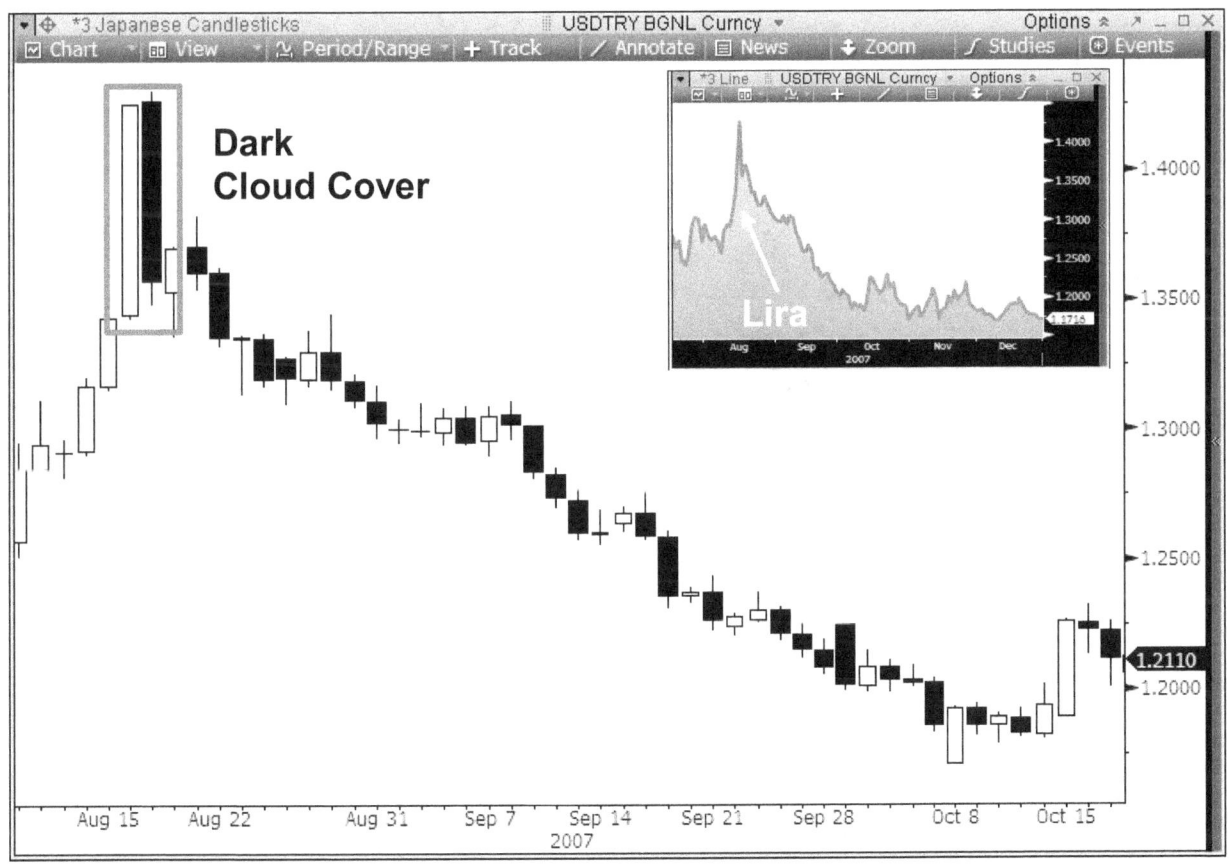

Fig 10. Dark Cloud Cover pattern forms at the peak of a rally, and at the impetus of a downward trend.

CANDLESTICK PATTERNS: Two Session

Tweezer Top/Tweezer Bottom

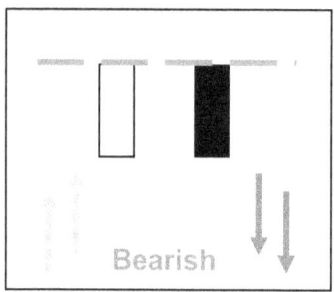

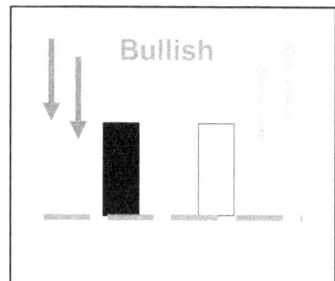

Signal
- Tweezer bottom signals a short term bullish reversal.
- Tweezer top signals a short term bearish reversal.

Criteria
- Two consecutive days in which either the high or the low are equal to each other. The color of the candle is of no relevance and the tweezers can be composed of real bodies, shadows, and/or doji. Ideally long first body, small second real body.

Implication
- Two consecutive highs or lows indicate a support or resistance is in place. Whatever force the market had on the first session is dissolving in the second. Particularly important pattern in weekly/monthly charts.

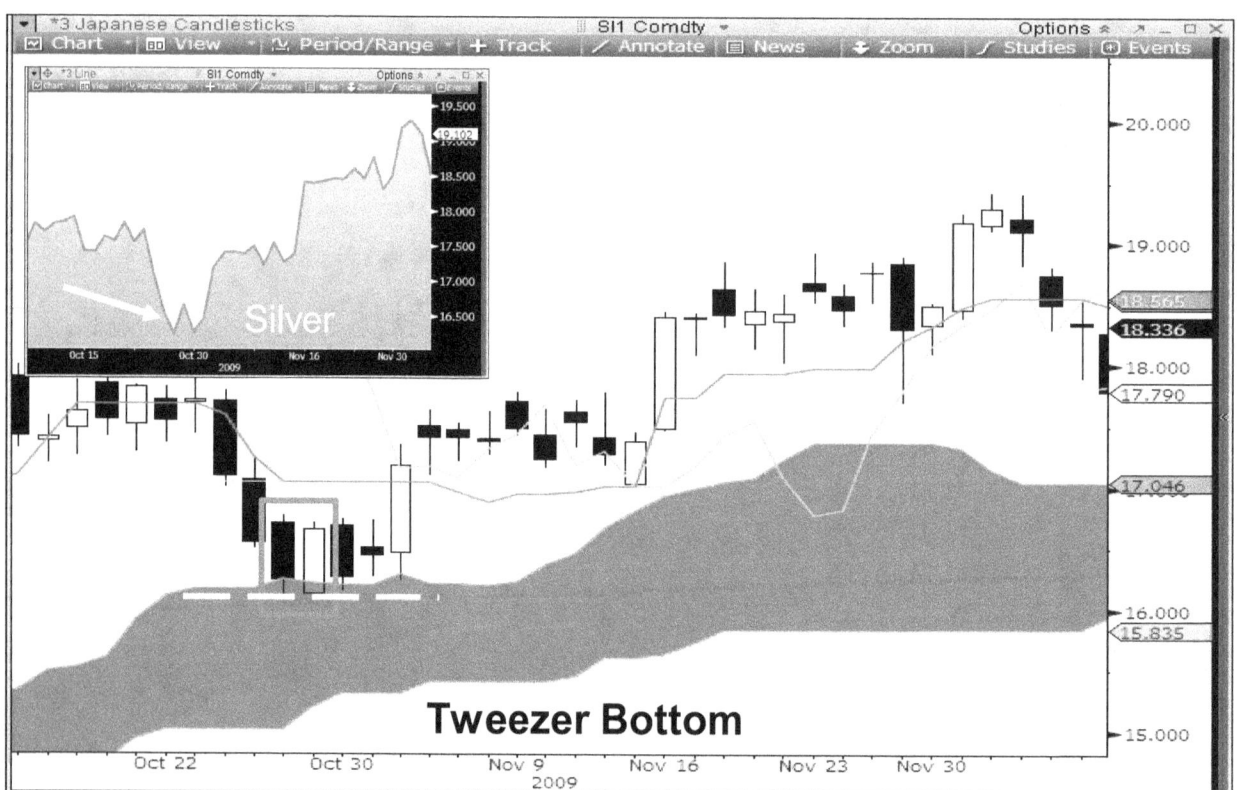

Fig 11. Silver future makes a Tweezer Bottom just above the upper boundary of the Ichimoku cloud, signalling a bullish reversal. Shortly thereafter, price passes through both Base and Conversion Lines, setting up for a strong upward bias.

CANDLESTICK PATTERNS: Three Session

Morning Star (Sankawa Ake No Myojyo)

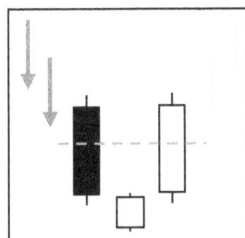

Signal
- Bullish reversal.

Criteria
- Must be located within a downtrend.
- Long bearish candle appears at the end of a downtrend. The following session has a small range and tends to gap lower. This is followed by a bullish long candle which rallies more than 50% of the recent bearish candle.

Implication
- Downtrend was dominant force, enticing prices to gap lower. However, the following small session symbolizes a potential change in sentiment. In astrology the Morning star planet "Mercury" appears before sunrise". Ultimately, the third session confirms and pushes higher.

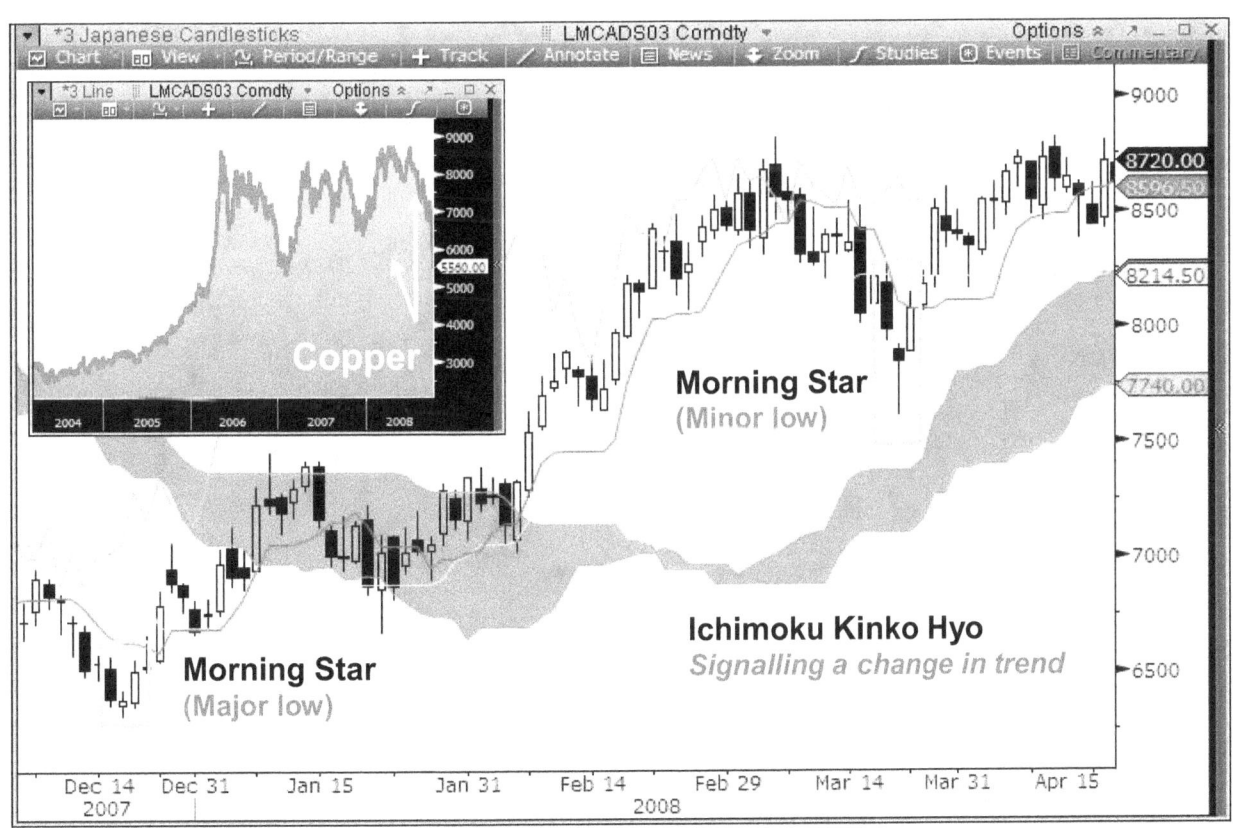

Fig 12. Morning star reversals at major and minor lows on Copper, with Ichimoku Kinko Hyo signalling a change in trend.

CANDLESTICK PATTERNS: Three Session

Evening Star (Sankawa Yoi No Myojyo)

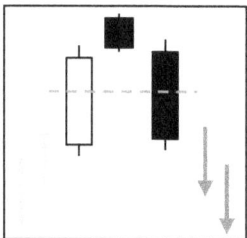

Signal
- Bearish reversal signal when found in an uptrend.

Criteria
- Must be located within an uptrend.
- Long bullish candle evident at end of uptrend. The following session has a small range and tends to gap higher. This is followed by a bearish long candle which falls more than 50% within the recent bullish candle.

Implication
- Uptrend was dominant force, enticing prices to gap higher. However, the following small session symbolizes a potential change in sentiment. In astrology the evening star planet "Venus" appears before night. Ultimately, the third session confirms and pushes lower.

Fig 13. A series of evening star reversal's during the top formation on S&P500 Index. Lower axis shows the RSI momentum indicator confirming bearish divergence, as upside momentum weakens.

CANDLESTICK PATTERNS: Three Session

Upside-Gap Two Crows

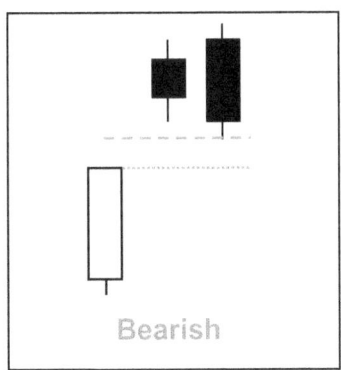

Bearish

Signal
- Bearish pattern indicating a topside reversal.

Criteria
- First session is a long white candle, followed by a black body gapped up. The pattern is completed by a third black candle which engulfs the body of the first day.

Implication
- The market is in an uptrend and gaps up to a new high. The market fails to hold this height, and follows by two black bodies, increasing in length. The sellers slowly begin to take control. If in the fourth session price fails to regain strength, the downside may prevail.

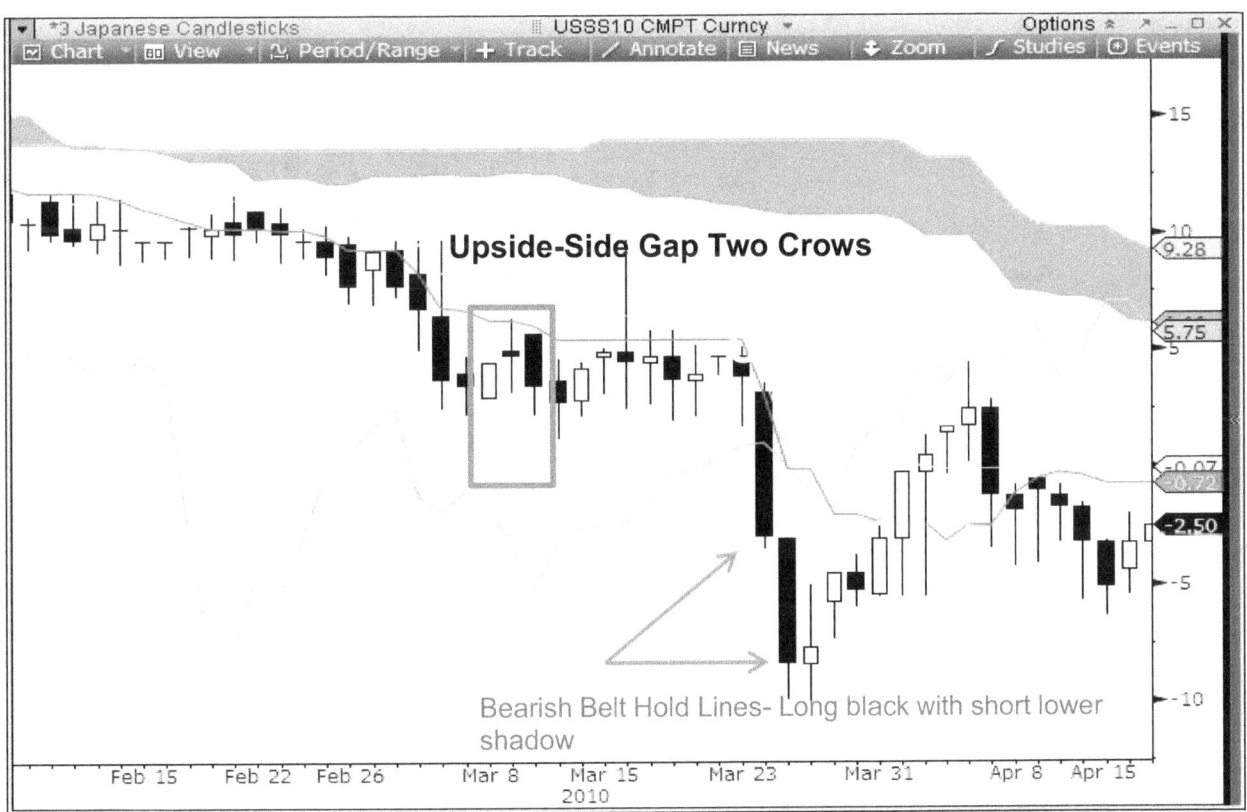

Fig 14. The US 10 year swap spreads display an upside gap two crows, forewarning of an imminent dip, which manifest only one week later in the form of two consecutive bearish candlesticks, further confirming the upside exhaustion.

CANDLESTICK PATTERNS: Three Session

Three White Soldiers

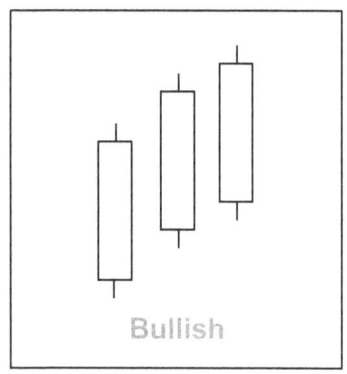
Bullish

Signal
- Bullish pattern signaling strength after a down trend or range-bound market.

Criteria
- Three consecutive sessions of long white candlesticks, each closing at or near previous high. Each candle begins at or near the range of the body of the previous.

Implication
- The Three White Soldiers imply a gradual and steady rise; a healthy market rise. If candles are overextended, one should be cautious of overbought conditions. If second or third shows weakness, possible Advance Block pattern.

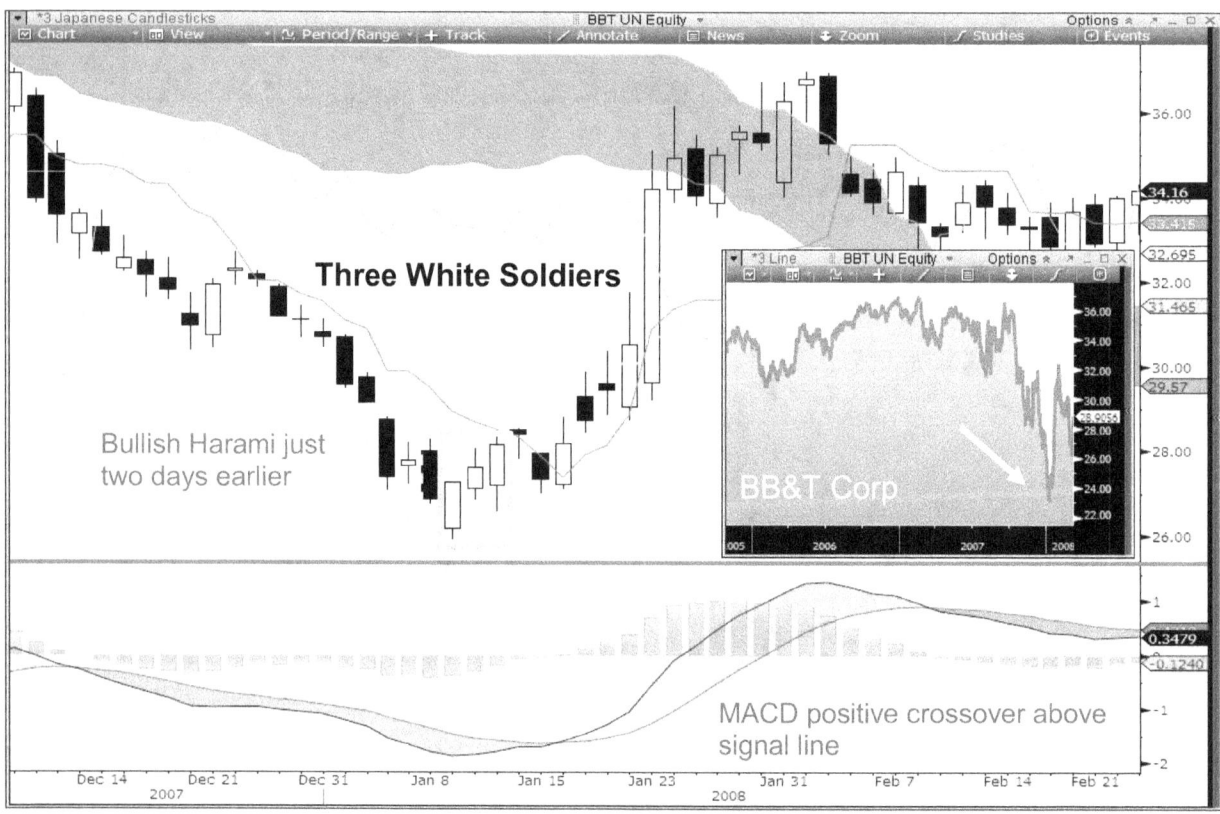

Fig 15. BB&T first signals a reversal of the previous downtrend with a bullish harami (small white, following an engulfing white). Subsequently, a three white soldier pattern emerges further indicating a shift in momentum to the upside, and again confirmed by a positive crossover in MACD.

CANDLESTICK PATTERNS: Three Session

Three Black Crows

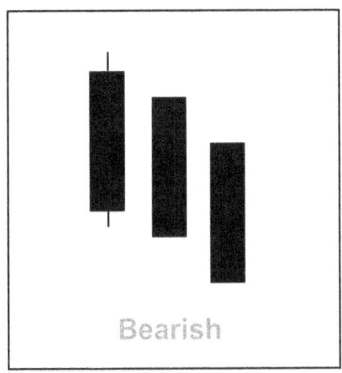

Signal
- Bearish pattern indicative of market correction.

Criteria
- Three consecutive sessions of long black candlesticks, each closing lower than the previous, each at or near their lows. Consecutive candles begin within the range of the body of the previous candle.

Implication
- The Three Black Crows pattern indicates a turn to strong selling pressure. The shadows are generally small and the bodies long. Pattern best suited for longer term traders who will watch for the completion of all three to take confirmation of market correction.

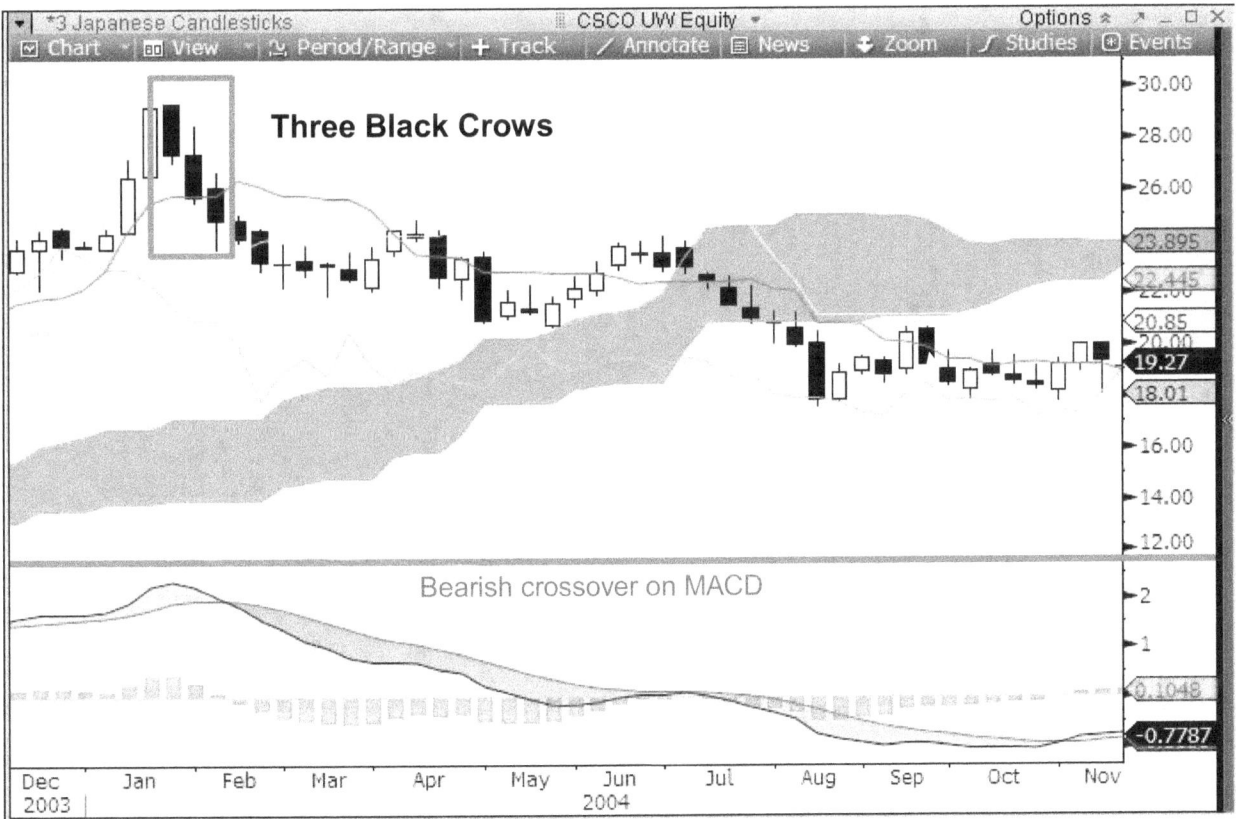

Fig 16. Three Black Crows forewarn of downside prevalence on CISCO as MACD crosses through the signal line and plummets past the zero point level.

CANDLESTICK PATTERNS: Three Session
Tasuki Gap

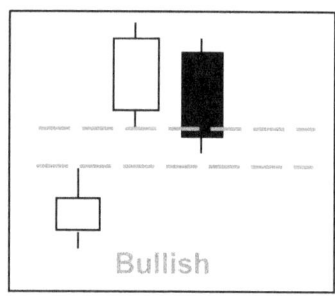

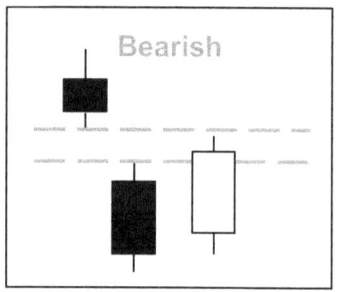

Signal
- Bullish continuation when tasuki gaps up.
- Bearish continuation when tasuki gaps down.

Criteria
- Bullish tasuki gaps up, then is followed by one white and one black candle, preferably similar in size. The second black candle opens within the real body and closes below. The opposite is true for a bearish tasuki gap.

Implication
- The gap does not get filled completely in the third session indicating that the prevailing trend will continue. However, should the gap be filled, support or resistance will have been broken and the bullish or bearish sentiment is thus voided.

Fig 17. In the above chart, price pushes down, into the ichimoku cloud, attempting to penetrate through, then pulls back momentarily with a series of white candlesticks filling the previous session"s gap.

CANDLESTICK PATTERNS:
Three Session

Gapping Side-by-Side White Lines

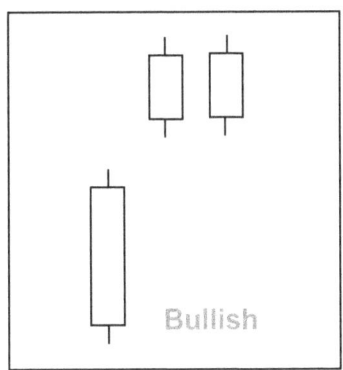

Signal
- Bullish continuation pattern.

Criteria
- First session is generally a long white candlestick, followed by an open above the close of the first candlestick. The following second and third sessions are similar in size, and both white.
- The close of the third session does not close the gap created between the first and second session.

Implication
- This pattern has the greatest relevance in an upward trend. In an already bullish environment, this pattern implies a continuation of the positive bias.

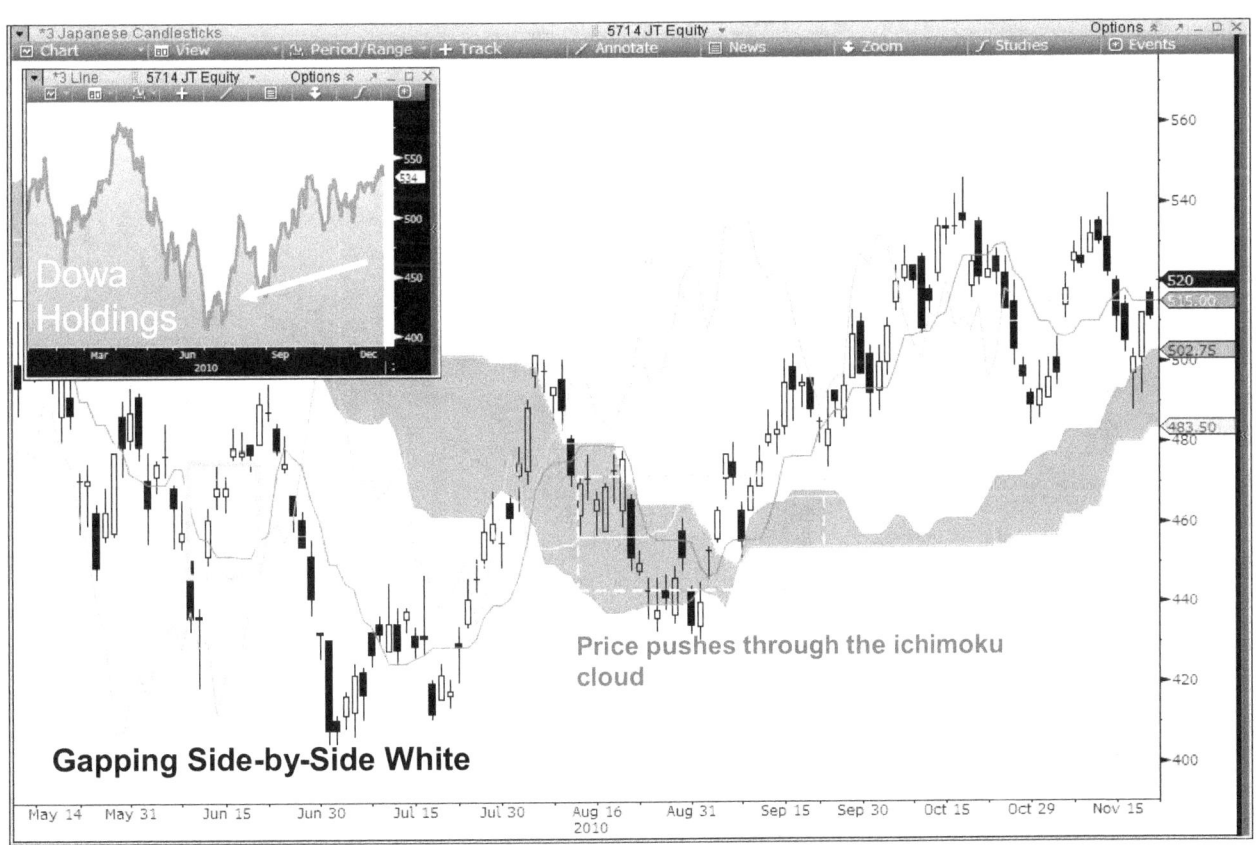

Fig 18. The IBEX breaks through the ichimoku cloud in a persistent bear trend, pauses for three short white inside bars, then resumes on heavy volume and long black bodies.

25

CANDLESTICK PATTERNS:
Three Session

Advance Block

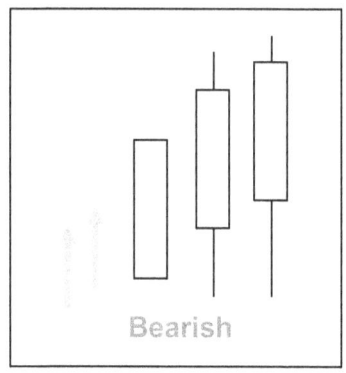

Signal
- Bearish reversal signal which appears at the top of a clear uptrend.

Criteria
- Three white candlesticks, similar to three white soldiers however the advance block always appears in an uptrend.
- The second and third sessions open within the body of the preceding session, and generally have long upper shadows.

Implication
- The previous uptrend is losing steam as each successive bull candle is weaker than the previous. The market is pushing for unsustainable highs and the shadows are showing lack of position strength.

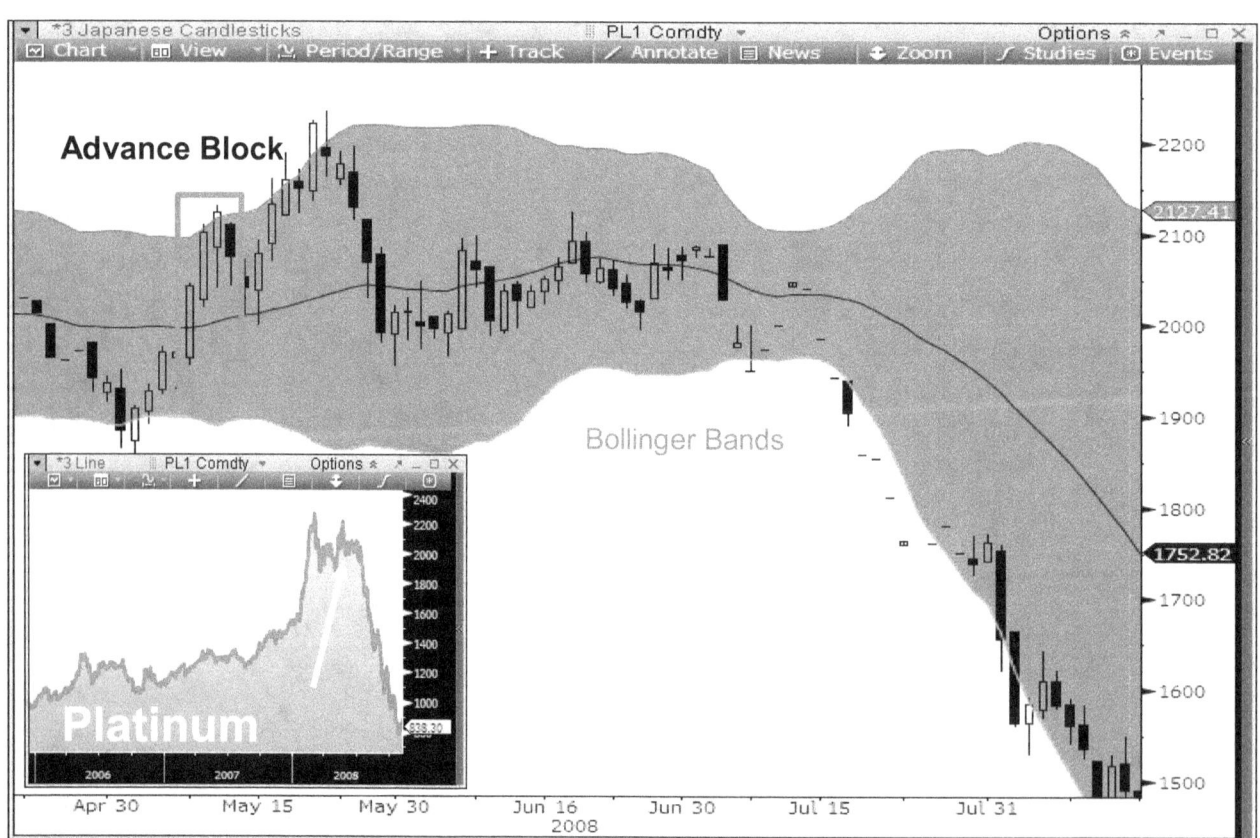

Fig 19. Platinum struggles to make new highs towards the end of a strong uptrend. Each new candle opens within the previous candle"s body, and closes on smaller and smaller body lengths. The failure swing made on the upper Bollinger band confirms a top is made and a reversal is imminent.

CANDLESTICK PATTERNS: Three Session

Abandoned Baby

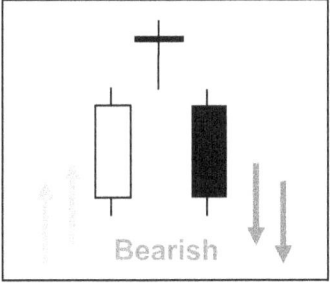

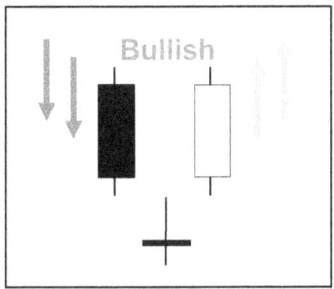

Signal
- Bullish reversal when found in a downtrend.
- Bearish reversal when found in an uptrend.

Criteria
- Must be located within their respective trends.
- Second session is a doji which gaps in the direction of the trend, followed by a third session which again gaps but in the opposite direction of the first session.

Implication
- Trend strength gaps in one last attempt, then a swift change in momentum pulls price in the opposing direction.

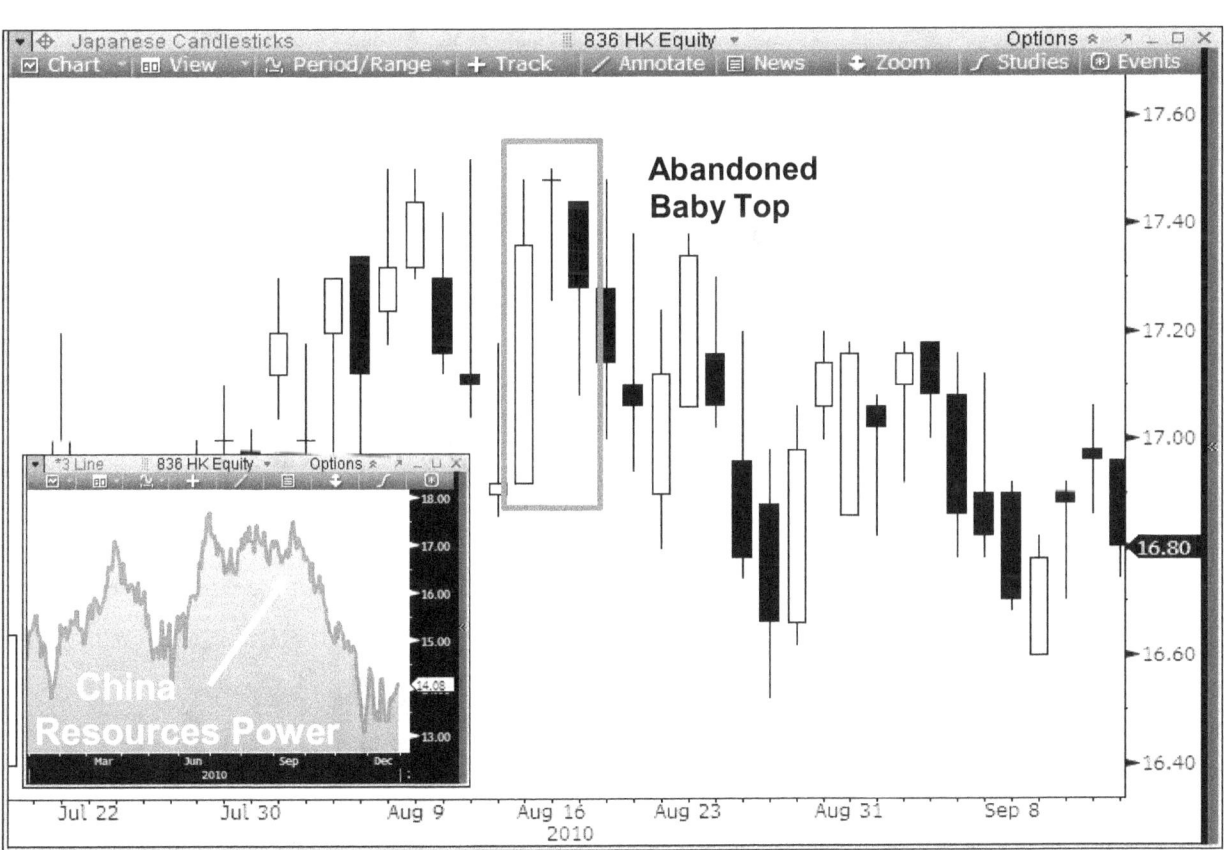

Fig 20. Abandoned baby top is a rare bearish signal, indicating an exhausted trend and a high probability reversal.

CANDLESTICK PATTERNS: Multiple Session

Rising Three Method/Falling Three Method

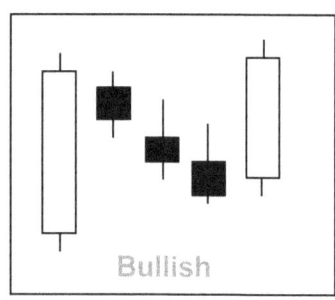
Bullish

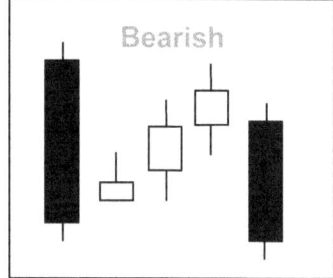
Bearish

Signal
- Bullish continuation when "rising".
- Bearish continuation when "falling".

Criteria
- First session is in the direction of the trend, followed by a series of 2-3 short bodied sessions ideally trading in the opposite direction of the trend, within the high to low range of the first candle. Finally a long body session resumes the direction of the prior trend.

Implication
- Three Method is considered a rest from trading, a rest from battle. Similar to a flag or pennant formation in Western chart patterns. Volume is ideally highest on the first and last candlesticks.

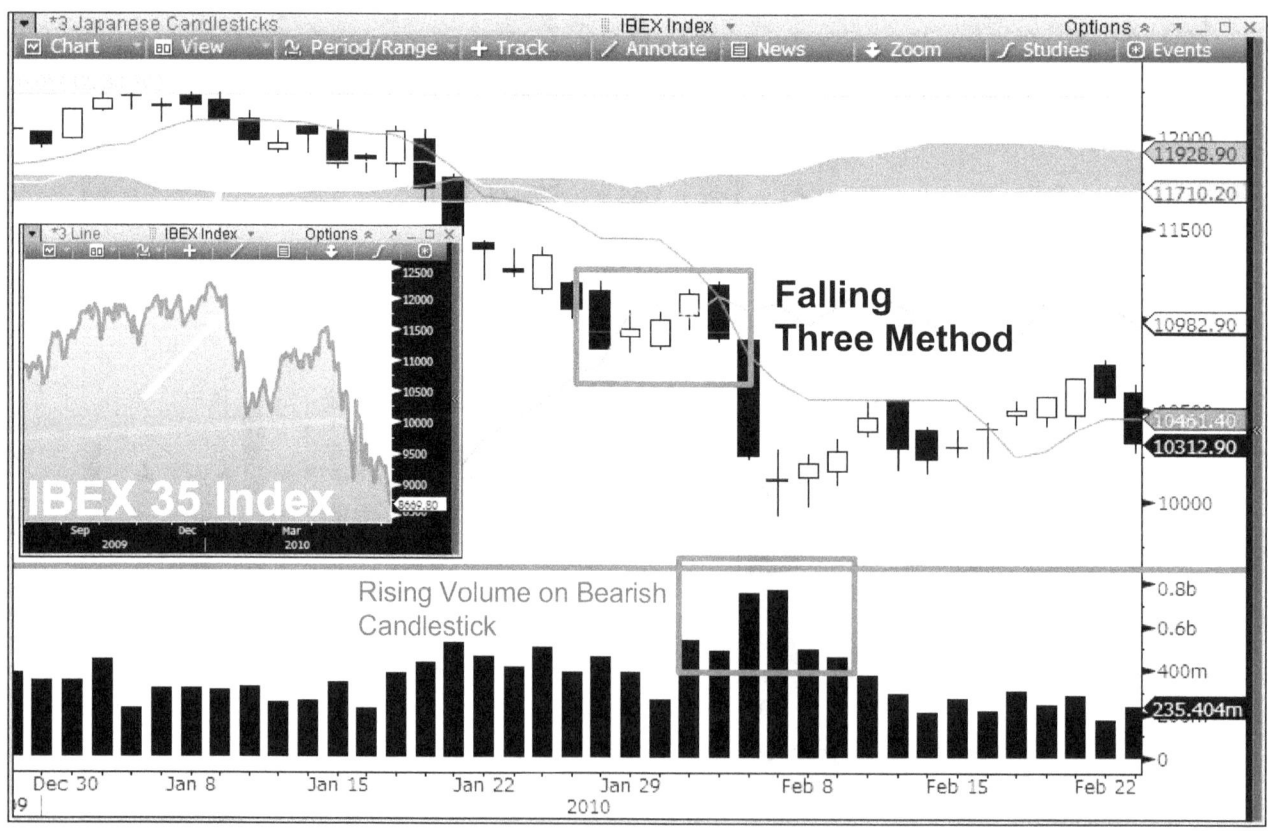

Fig 21. The IBEX breaks through the ichimoku cloud in a persistent bear trend, pauses for three short white inside bars, then resumes on heavy volume and long black bodies.

SUMMARY: *Japanese* Candlesticks „Cheat Sheet"

One Session

Long Bullish/Bearish
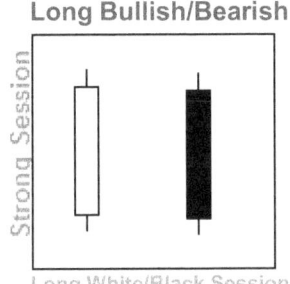
Long White/Black Session
"Strong Session"

Doji
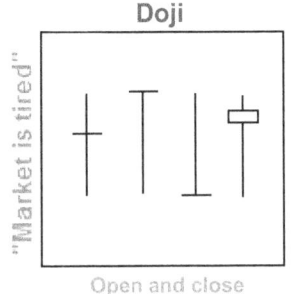
Open and close are narrow or same
"Market is tired"

Spinning Top
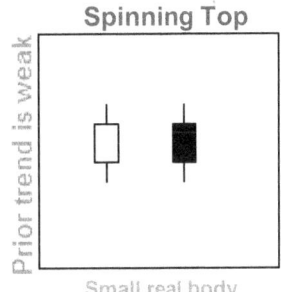
Small real body
Prior trend is weak

High Wave
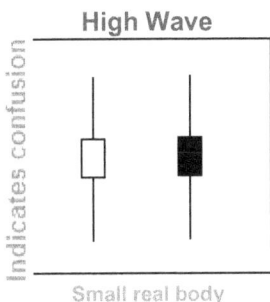
Small real body
Long Shadows
Indicates confusion

Hammer
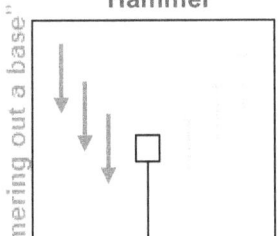
Lower Shadow twice the length of Real Body which is at the top range
"Hammering out a base"

Inverted Hammer
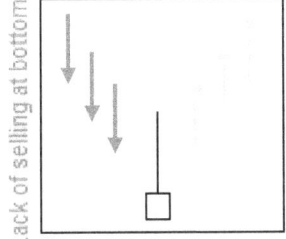
Upper Shadow twice the length of Real Body which is at the bottom range
"Lack of selling at bottom"

Shooting Star
SAME as Inverted Hammer
TOP REVERSAL SIGNAL
"Trouble overhead"

Hanging Man
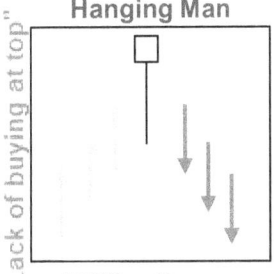
SAME as Hammer
TOP REVERSAL SIGNAL
"Lack of buying at top"

Two Session

Engulfing
Large Real Body wraps Around small Real Body
Must be opposite colours
"Arresting control"

Harami
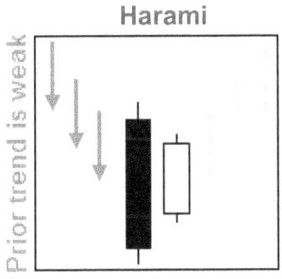
Small Real Body contained inside Large Real Body
Must be opposite colours
Prior trend is weak

Piercing Line
Downtrend evident
Session opens < prior low
White RB cls >50% into Black
Postv sentiment reversal

Dark Cloud Cover
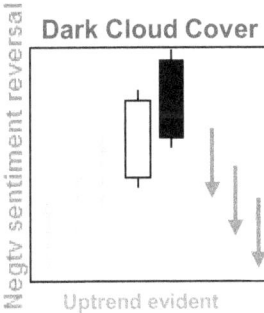
Uptrend evident
Session opens > prior high
Black RB cls >50% into White
Negtv sentiment reversal

Three Session

Morning Star
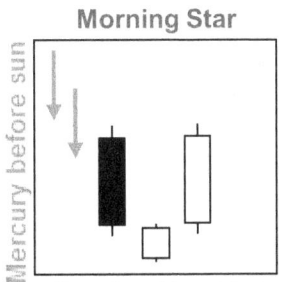
Downtrend is evident
Black candle followed by star
White candle cls >50% into Prior black candle
Mercury before sun

Evening Star
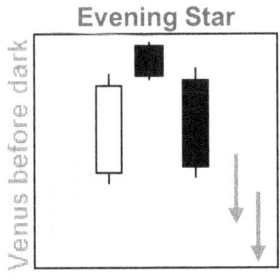
Uptrend is evident
White candle followed by star
Black candle cls >50% into
Venus before dark

Three White Soldiers
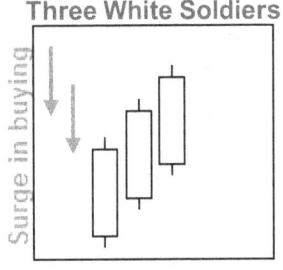
Downtrend is evident
3 White RB's, all similar size
Each session cls near high
Surge in buying

Three Black Crows
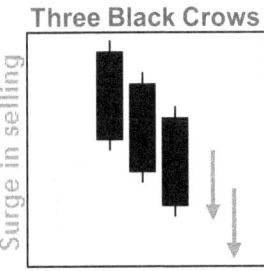
Uptrend evident
3 Black RB's, all similar size
Each session cls near low
Surge in selling

SUMMARY: Japanese Candlestick - Frequently Asked Questions

Q1. How do you differentiate between a bullish and bearish candle?
There are many different combinations of colours that people use to code candlestick patterns. Most popular are black/white and red/green. Sometimes it's best not to think of the colour coding of a candlestick and instead examine its construction logic. (See page 6).

For example, a bullish (positive) session is where the market rises and closes higher < than it opens. This means that buyers maintained control. The opposite is true for a bearish (negative) session where the market falls and closes lower > than its opening price.

Q2. What is the importance of the candlestick „real body" and shadow?
Japanese candlestick analysts believe the rectangle section of a candlestick, otherwise known as the "real body" is "the essence of market psychology", where the overall commitment is held. Meanwhile, shadows, which are the thin vertical lines (candle „wick") are the extreme price ranges for the session. They are also important and symbolize a yin-yang relationship. They indicate that momentum has been offset.

Q3. What key principles should be used to confirm a candlestick signal?
It"s important to find a confluence of signals to provide the trade setup, thereby increasing the probability of a candlestick pattern's success. This is where Eastern methods meet with Western, compounding basic filters like trend, momentum to more sophisticated Ichimoku Kinko Hyo or Demark Indicators.

Thereafter, it's advised to wait for price continuation and confirmation above a specific area before triggering a trade decision. Finally, each signal should offer an attractive risk/reward profile, so to ensure profitable longevity in the financial market.

Q4. What are the best timeframes to use candlesticks?
The great thing about Japanese candlesticks is they can be applied to all timeframes. In fact, by using multiple timeframes to confirm signals, we can significantly increase their success rate. At the s/t scale, 15 min intraday charts tend to be reliable, helping sharpen entry/exit points and for l/t confirmations, weekly charts are good. The most key proponents are mass psychology, liquidity and underline volatility.

Q5. How do candlesticks differ between markets?
There are subtle differences in characteristic between markets. These range from a market"s unique volatility characteristic (which impacts the size of a candlestick) to the session"s open and close defaults.

This is most notable in the FX market where trading hours span 24hrs in three different time zones. On the major currency pairs, most are divided into the following three camps on which close to choose; i) simply defaulting to domestic region e.g. USA/Europe/Asia. ii) Using a strategic FX close that is impacted greatly by major economic events (this tends to be US centric). iii) Superior FX volume. London trading accounts for 31% of total FX volume. Where as the US only accounts for 19% FX volume.

Q6. Which indicators should be used to confirm candlestick signals?
To achieve a high probability of success it is best to choose a diversity of non-correlated indicators with a proven track record. One example would be to start with a momentum study that measures overbought/oversold extremes, such as RSI or Stochastics. This is because the majority of candlestick signals are „reversal" oriented and so indicators that anticipate reversals would work best.

Q7. How accurate are candlestick signals?
There have been several back-tested studies on the accuracy of candlestick signals. Results tend to vary and will of course depend on the chosen candle criteria, risk and money management profiles applied. Ultimately, Japanese candlestick analysis is seen as a strategic trading technique and not a system.

www.ingramcontent.com/pod-product-compliance
Lightning Source LLC
Chambersburg PA
CBHW080439220526
45465CB00009B/3351